Circus Tricks

Ruth Komesaroff
Illustrated by Lisa Coutts

Contents

Circus Kids	2
Acrobat	3
Juggler	5
Clown	7
Trick Cyclist	9
Tightrope Walker	11
Trapeze Artist	13
Match the Pictures	15

Circus Kids

Welcome to the circus!
Children do clever tricks here.
So step right up. Enjoy the show!

Acrobat

I'm an acrobat.
I do backflips.

On circus night...

3

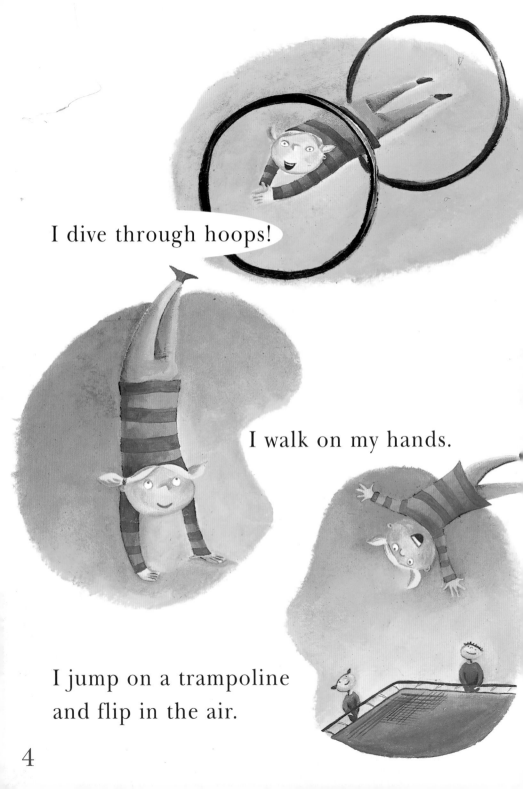

I dive through hoops!

I walk on my hands.

I jump on a trampoline
and flip in the air.

4

Juggler

I'm a juggler.
I juggle balls, rings, and clubs.

On circus night...

I juggle a lot of balls.

I spin a top along some rope.

Then I throw the top in the air and catch it.

Clown

I'm a clown.
I tell funny jokes.

On circus night...

7

I trip over
my big shoes
and fall down a lot.

I tell
funny jokes

I shout and yell
and act silly.

8

Trick Cyclist

I'm a trick cyclist.
I do tricks on bikes.

On circus night...

I ride a bike backward.

I ride a bike
with one wheel.

I do a handstand on a bike.

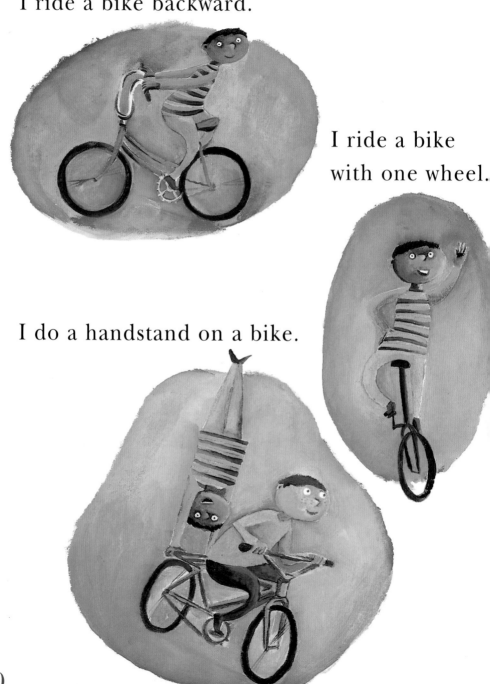

Tightrope Walker

I'm a tightrope walker.
I walk in the air on a wire.

On circus night...

11

I jump and hop along the wire.

I do the splits on the wire.

I skip along the wire
with a jump rope.

Trapeze Artist

I'm a trapeze artist.
I swing and hang upside down.

On circus night...

I swing upside down
and hang by my toes.

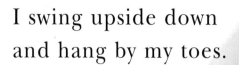

I swing through the air
and let go of the trapeze.

Another trapeze artist swings
and catches me.

Match the Pictures

What do the circus kids use?
Can you match the pictures?

That's better!
Now the circus kids can do their tricks.

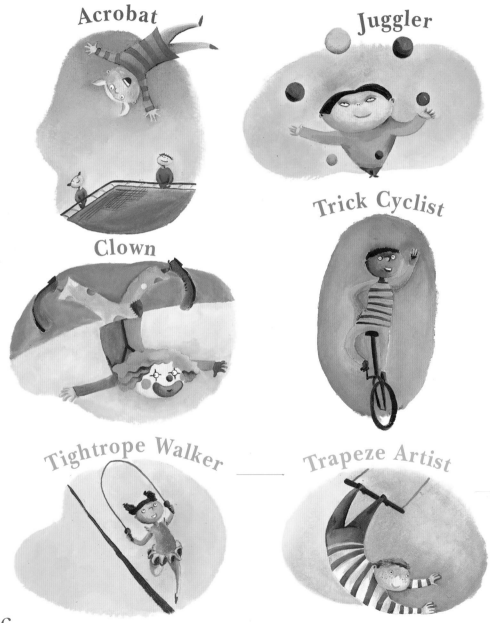

Acrobat

Juggler

Trick Cyclist

Clown

Tightrope Walker

Trapeze Artist